STUKA!

Joachim Dressel

▲ 1 ▼ 2

1. The Junkers K 47 was designed in 1928 by Dipl.-Ing. Plauth at AB Flygindustri in Sweden. The building of aircraft was forbidden by the victorious Allies after the First World War. The K 47 was conceived as an all-metal two-seat version of a fighter aircraft, related to the Dessau-produced A 48 training and experimental aircraft. The K 47 was powered by a 550hp BMW VII, or by a Bristol Jupiter. Some of the Junkers K 47 were sold to China, two more found their way to the USSR where Junkers became very useful in developing a modern Russian air force.

STUKA!

Joachim Dressel

ARMS AND
ARMOUR

2. The military version of the Junkers K 47 took part in early experiments in low-level and dive-bombing attack. The 540hp powered aircraft was less successful. In October 1930 the 'Swedish' K 47 was shown on the ground and in flight by one of the best pilots, delighting a large audience at Bucharest. But there is no proof that the local air force was authorized to buy some of the double-fin, multi-purpose aircraft. Only the first prototype, with a central rudder, was flown. Because of the different position of the rear armament, the Junkers A 47 was fitted with a different tail-plane and rudder configuration.

3. A few months before the beginning of the Second World War the modified K 47s were handed over to Luftwaffe training units in central Germany. The rear armament was rebuilt to modify the few existing aircraft to normal two-seat trainers; one of these took part in trials by the Luftwaffe staff to test the 'Stuka Idea'.

4. In 1936 the technical office of the Reichsluftfahrtministerium (RLM) ordered the four major aircraft developers to start work on developing an experimental dive-bomber, the Stuka, and a low-level attacker, the Schlachtflugzeug, whose role would be to clear the way for fast motorized forces. The *'Blitzkrieg'* became familiar to all European nations only a few years later. Besides Blohm & Voss, Heinkel and Junkers, the Arado works began the lay-out and construction of single or two-seat aircraft with a powerful piston engine. The Ar 81 V3 was the first fast biplane experimental Stuka with a rear armament.

▲ 3   ▼ 4

INTRODUCTION

First published in Great Britain in
1989 by Arms and Armour Press,
Artillery House, Artillery Row,
London SW1P 1RT.

Distributed in the USA by Sterling
Publishing Co. Inc., 387 Park
Avenue South, New York,
NY 10016-8810.

Distributed in Australia by
Capricorn Link (Australia) Pty. Ltd.,
P.O. Box 665, Lane Cove, New
South Wales 2066, Australia.

British Library Cataloguing in
Publication Data:
Dressel, Joachim
Stuka! – (Warbirds fotofax)
1. World War 2. Air operations by
Germany. Luftwaffe. Junkers Stuka
aeroplanes
   Title II. Series
940.54'4943
ISBN 0-85368-907-5

Designed and edited by DAG
Publications Ltd. Designed by
David Gibbons; edited by Michael
Boxall; layout by David Gibbons;
typeset by Ronset Typesetters Ltd,
Darwen, Lancashire, and by
Typesetters (Birmingham) Limited,
Warley, West Midlands;
camerawork by M&E
Reproductions, North Fambridge,
Essex; printed and bound in Great
Britain by The Alden Press Limited,
Oxford.

Influenced by the years of trench warfare during the First World War the German Supreme Staff sought new ways of waging war, including the use of overwhelming air support for their ground forces. Besides destroying the enemy's troops behind the front line, communication installations and traffic routes were proposed as major targets.

A development of the fast medium aircraft, e.g., the He 111 and Ju 88, the smaller Ju 87 'Stuka' (Stuka is a contraction of Sturzkampf, meaning dive-bombing) would become the spearhead of a system that would enable the fully armoured panzer divisions to *Blitzkrieg* their way through an opposing army. The Stukas played the principal role in the successful deep penetration and resultant disorganization which undermined the enemy's ability to resist or counter-attack. Together with the 8.8cm Flak, the Stukas cleared the front lines wherever Polish or French tank forces posed a threat to German armour.

The first tests were undertaken secretly during the 1920s, with Russian assistance, at Lipetzk. Modern dive-bombers were later developed thanks to neutral countries, notably Sweden and Switzerland, who helped accelerate the illegal formation of the Luftwaffe. At this time the Americans and the Japanese were engaged in practical trials of dive-bombing against fortifications and ships. The Curtiss Hawk, purchased by Ernst Udet and tested by the Luftwaffe, inspired the Luftwaffenführung who ordered their first two-seat dive-bomber, the He 50.

Hans Jeschonnek, the commanding chief of the Luftwaffe General Staff, and Wolfram von Richthofen, the technical head in the newly created Technische Amt of the Reichsluftfahrtministerium, supported nearly all of Udet's proposals. New aircraft were built by Arado and Blohm & Voss, but neither the Ar 81 nor the Ha 137 had a real chance of mass production following the appearance of the Junkers Ju 87 Stuka.

The first units were soon established. Following the IV (Stuka)/LG1, the first Gruppe (or Wing) of Stukageschwader 1 (shortened to StG) was raised. (A Geschwader was the equivalent of an RAF Group.) Later, the Luftwaffe formed the II and III StG2 and the 4 (Stuka)/186; after these, more and more Stuka-Gruppen began to undergo intensive training in Central Germany.

The first major operations came a short time later: Poland surrendered a few days after eight Stuka-Gruppen had bombarded Warsaw. The Ju 87 had created its legendary reputation. The invasions of Denmark, Norway, the Netherlands, Belgium and France were the prelude to bloody Stuka attacks against British targets. From then on the Ju 87B operated over a region where Germany did not have air superiority; heavy losses were the result and the dive-bombers were removed. In the North African and Russian theatres of war the Stuka units were responsible for many victories despite great setbacks themselves; it was here that the Stuka evolved into a Schlactflugzeug or ground-attacker and tank-buster.

I should like to express my sincere thanks to several friends who helped with new photographs and data: Messrs. Arena, Bekker, Dabrowski, Emmerling, Francella, Mohr, Koos, Ing Prevsdiken, Reck, Selinger and Zobel. My special thanks go to Mr. Griehl for his great help and Mr. Radinger for his colour illustrations.

▲ 5

▲ 6 ▼ 7

5. The Blohm & Voss concept, the Ha 137, revealed a single-seat metal Stuka which was powered by a Jumo 210 C, the same engine used with the Ar 81 experimentals. The aircraft carried one 20mm cannon and two 7.9mm MG 17. It was possible to load one 250kg bomb under the centreline, and four small SC 50 bombs under the outer wing sections. Only five Ha 137s, one of them D-IUXU, were built by the Hamburger Flugzeugbau after the mock-up was accepted by the RLM in October 1934.

6. In the fuselage of the fourth prototype Ha 137V4, D-IFOE, a Jumo 210 A-1 engine of 610hp was fitted by Blohm & Voss. Colonel von Richthofen proposed producing the Ha 137 in large quantities, but Ernst Udet, who became the Generalluftzeugmeister and was responsible for all kinds of development of new aircraft for the Luftwaffe, decided to cancel the Blohm & Voss aircraft even though the flight behaviour was very good and the conversions showed an improved armament consisting of two 20mm cannon and two MG 17.

7. The He 118 was one of the 'Günter designs'. The Günter brothers were famous aircraft designers who designed nearly all Heinkel aircraft. Siegfried was responsible for the He 51, He 70, He 100, He 111, He 114, He 115, He 119, He 177 and the He 219. His brother Walter developed the He 64, the fast He 70, the jet and rocket experimentals He 176 and He 178 and the heavy He 118 Stuka. After the Heinkel proposal of the early He 50, dive-bombers were only built in small quantities. The two-seat He 118 is very interesting when compared to the eventual Stuka. The He 118 D-OQYF was the third pre-series aircraft (Nullserien Flugzeug).

8. The Henschel Hs 123 flew for the first time on 8 May 1935. The experimental 'Henschel Stuka' was constructed without any official permission. Ernst Udet, who had purchased some

8 ▲

Curtiss Hawks in the USA, was present at the first take-off and followed the first diving trials with great interest. It seemed that the Technisches Amt of the RLM would order large quantities of the Hs 123 (also called 'Henschel one-two-three'), but when the Luftwaffe decided to build the Junkers Stuka there was little room for the old Hs 123 just one year later.

9. At the Junkers aircraft works at Dessau the drafting bureau had been engaged in constructing a powerful Stuka design since the autumn of 1933, initiated by Dipl.-Ing. Pohlmann who was one of the 'Old Eagles' of the First World War, an experienced flier. After developing the Junkers A/K 47 and 48 with its double fin section, the first Ju 87 became the principal of its period. The wooden mock-up was finished during the winter of 1934–5 and shown to commissioners from Berlin, who controlled all progress concerning the Stuka development.

9 ▼

▲ 10

▲ 11 ▼ 12

10. The Junkers technicians started construction of the first prototype, the Junkers Ju 87 V1 at the Dessau works. In the spring of 1936 the new spearhead of the coming *Blitzkrieg* appeared. Its gull-shaped wings would become a menacing shadow over European battlefields. The double tail section did not become a regular feature since the performance during the div phase was too high for that concept. In addition, the first flight trials of the early Ju 87 in the mid-thirties showed some minor problems of stability.

11. This photograph was taken just before the first take-off on 17 September 1935. Despite its ungainly appearance, the Junkers bomber showed relatively smooth handling characteristics. The unique floating flaps designed by the Junkers team, and the ailerons, contributed to lightness of control. The first prototype was powered by a Rolls-Royce Kestrel V driving a two-bladed, fixed-pitch wooden propeller. It undertook many evaluation trials in central Germany durin the summer of 1935.

12. This photograph of the first Junkers Ju 87 V1 was taken at Dessau during servicing of the engine. Although the prototype had been designed to accommodate air brakes, they were not fitted before preliminary tests, and excessive vibration during the dive cause the double tail section to break away and the prototype crashed Only a very few modifications were necessary to the fuselage, wings and undercarriage, but the tail unit was altered to a central fin and new dive brakes were fitted by Junkers specialists.

13. The third prototype Ju 87 V3, coded D-UKYQ, during a fly-past at Dessau. After modifying the second Stuka, the Ju 87 V3 was equipped with the under-wing dive brakes which enabled the aircraft to dive at an angle of 90°. During several flight trials in June and July 1936, the Ju 87 overcame its main rivals the Ar 81 and He 118. The latter, the first monoplane dive-bomber, with a retractable undercarriage and powered by a 900hp DB 600A piston engine had no real chance; both designs failing to achieve larger dive angles than 50° or 55°.

14. The D-UBIP was submitted to several tests by the Luftwaffe. It was the fourth Ju 87 to become the predecessor of the Ju 87 A-1 'Anton' series that was ordered after Udet's impulsive flying of the He 118 without have read the handbook. After the He 118's propeller was ripped off, Udet took to his parachute. Alone, he continued to advocate development of the Junkers dive-bomber. After fitting the powerful Jumo 210 A on the final prototype the refined aircraft received a squared-off vertical fin and a faired-in after canopy. In order to clear the dropped bomb away from the larger propeller arc, a special forward-swinging rack was fitted beneath the forward fuselage.

15. Despite the criticism of the dive-bombing idea, Udet ordered the building of the ten Ju 87 A-O of the first pre-production batch. The early Stukas had an average maximum speed of only 200mph approximately, and the normal military payload was reduced to a single SC 250 bomb. When using the SC 500 bomb it was impossible to carry a rear-facing gunner. The first production models entered service with I./Sturzkampfgeschwader 162 'Immelmann' during the spring of 1937.

13 ▲

14 ▲   15 ▼

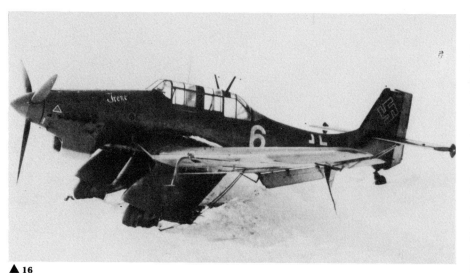

▲ 16

▲ 17   ▼ 18

16. Werknummer 5010 was one of the first Junkers Ju 87 A-1 aircraft. Here the name of the pilot's bride 'Irene' can be seen on a panel covering the Jumo 210 A which was later replaced by the more powerful Jumo 211. The biplanes flown by the first Stuka Gruppen were withdrawn and handed over to one of the several training units.

17. A side view of a Ju 87 A-1 operating near Barcelona with the Condor Legion during the Spanish Civil War. Four fully equipped Stukas were flown by Luftwaffe crews during the war. The camouflage of the 29-4 was green and brown in a common splinter pattern system. The Ju 87 A-1 were flown with an external bomb-rack comprising the Schlo 500 XIB for a maximum load of 500kg. Additionally these aircraft were armed with two MG 17 with 500 rounds and one defensive flexible MG 15 with 900 rounds operated by the rear-gunner. The roomy 'greenhouse' canopy gave an excellent all-round view and enabled the second man to defend the aircraft against enemy fighters.

18. The Ju 87 A-2 appeared late in 1937 featuring an uprated 680hp Jumo 210Da piston engine, together with a two-stage supercharger and improved communications equipment. Many of the Junkers Ju 87 A-1 were so modified, and had their upper rudder section rounded off too. These lined-up Stukas belonged to the Stukaschule indicated by the code L25 which meant the 25th aircraft of that training unit. The numbers before the Balkenkreuz showed the region where the school Gruppe was stationed.

19. Another Ju 87 A-2, one of the total of 262 Junkers Stukas built by the end of 1938 when the A-series was terminated by the RLM after the proposed successor of the Ju 87A, the Ju 87 B, was already under development by the Junkers Projektbüro. Of the 262 Ju 87 A-O, A-1 and A-2, 192 were built at the main plant at Dessau, the

others being produced by
Weserflugzeugbau near Bremen
and the Berlin-Tempelhof
assembly line.

20. A detailed view of an under-
fuselage bomb-rack, close to the
two support struts of the
undercarriage. A small window
afforded the pilot a view of the
landscape during horizontal
flight. Under the wing the dive
brake and one of the MG 17s
can be seen. Near the wing root
the small plate indicates the
name of the producer firm, the
year of manufacture and the
aircraft's weight.

21. The wing racks of the Ju 87 A-2, each with one SC 50 · demolition bomb. It was possible to fix up to 200kg in each of the Junkers' racks. Apart from the GP bombs, all kinds of fragmentation or incendiary bombs could be used under the wings of the Junkers Stuka.

▲ 21

22. A few Stukas were used for liaison missions and for medical purposes by dive-bomber units. This Ju 87 A-1 was the personal aircraft of the Stabsarzt for transporting one wounded or sick man. All weapons have been removed, there are no MG 17 in the wings and no bomb strong point under the fuselage. The sign was a symbol for Luftwaffe medical help, also found on the Fw 58 Weihe which was often used for important rescue missions.

 ▲ 22   ▼ 23

23, 24, 25. These three pictures show dummy Ju 87s in France after the German occupation in 1940. Luftwaffe personnel used French horse-drawn carts to transport the wooden Ju 87 fuselages. Near a little wood several mock-ups are being built and later will be camouflaged to indicate to an enemy reconnaissance aircraft an intact German airfield. Additionally some old trucks, tents and exercise bombs have been laid down beside the wooden 'Stukas' to imitate a Stuka Gruppe before the next attack against targets in the English Channel or the British Isles.

24 ▲

25 ▲   26 ▼

26. One of the early Junkers Ju 87 B-O pre-series prototypes during its evaluation at Dessau airfield, *circa* late summer of 1938. The unpainted aircraft is being balance tested. It differed from the Ju 87 A-1 and A-2 by having an altered fuselage, and some improvements to the greenhouse section. The rear-gunner had an additional duty, becoming responsible for operating the FuG VIIa radio installed behind the pilot's seat. The main landing gear was completely redesigned in order that heavier loads could be carried.

27. The D-IELX had been equipped with a new radiator on the front fuselage and a different air intake. The aircraft was painted in a standard splinter pattern and had the normal civil code in black letters and the black-and-white swastikas on a red background. During the first trials the early B-Stuka was still unarmed. The improvements in the cockpit's interior were the replaced Revi 12 bomb sight and a gun aiming reflector sight for the pilot.

28. A view showing mass production of the Ju 87 B-1 Stuka at Weserflugzeugbau near Bremen. More than thirty Ju 87s are under construction in the factory hall, the Längsschiff. One can notice different stages of completion of the inner wing sections and the fuselages. The fitting of the

Jumo 211 took place in another production row. The greenhouses are protected by tough canvas.

29. Ju 87 B-1 during the final checks by specialists of the Bauaufsicht Luft (BAL) at Dessau early in the war. The production number was still being painted in large white numerals on both sides of the fuselage. Of special interest during the check was the Jumo 211 piston engine with its cooling, electric and fuel systems. During the first flight trials the aircraft had civil codes and swastikas.

▲ 30   ▼ 31

30. Two Ju 87 B-1s during final maintenance work on the Jumo 211 AV engines. The Werknummern 209 and, in the foreground, 211 stand in front of the modern fabrication halls at Dessau. All engine coverings have been removed for checking engines and lower radiators. After that the Stukas were flown to the Frontschleuse, an air base, where the military installations were fitted by Luftwaffe personnel. The Stukas were then tested again before being handed over to front-line units called Stuka Geschwader.

31. Three Ju 87 B-1s in formation flown by pilots from Junkers. All three aircraft still have the production numbers painted on their sides. By the end of August 1939 more than 460 Ju 87s had been delivered to the Luftwaffe, enough to form nine Stuka Gruppen operated by parts of the Stuka Geschwader StG 1, 2, 51, 76 and 77. In addition an operational training unit, IV./Lehrgeschwader 1, and an experimental naval dive-bombing squadron were established.

32. A Fliegerdenkmal (memorial) of a Ju 87 B-1 of III. Gruppe of the Stukageschwader 2 'Immelmann', named after the famous German airman of the First World War. Many German front-line aircraft crashed on muddy airfields without hardcover runways and had to be repaired by the Feldwerftkompanien of the Luftwaffe in large tents, or without any covering, because of a lack of hangar capacity.

33. Three Junkers Stukas of the Nationalist Spanish Air Force in action over central Spain. The aircraft were painted in the new black-green, dark-green splinter camouflage. The undersides were sprayed light-blue.

34. An early front-line Stuka being serviced by a group of so-called 'Blackmen' (ground crew). While some take care of refuelling, others bring SC 50 bombs for the wing racks. In the foreground is a truck for transporting the SC 500, one of the standard GP bombs used by all Luftwaffe bomber and Stuka units.

32 ▲

33 ▲ 34 ▼

▲ 35 ▼ 36　　　　　　　　▼ 37

35. A Ju 87 B, production number 429, receives adjustment to the MG 17s in the wings while on active service in the west, possibly in France, in 1940.

36. In December 1939 the Ju 87 B-1 and B-2 began receiving the uprated 1,200hp Junkers Jumo 211 Da piston engine. The improved aircraft was designated B-2. The ejector exhausts and radiator bath cooling flaps were redesigned, eliminating the exterior hinging plates which were visible on the early B aircraft. To give an additional increase of airflow into the radiator to cool the more powerful engine, the mouth of the radiator bath was enlarged.

37, 38. A Ju 87 B-2 during final completion at the Dessau works. In the background Ju 88 bombers await their last installations. The dive brakes have been fixed under the wings and the racks for the centreline bomb-load have been installed.

38 ▲   39 ▼

39. This illustration of the main undercarriage unit, without coverings, is from the technical manual issued to trainee workers and Luftwaffe ground crew. There is a slit between the outer wing and the wing junctions of the Ju 87 B. The complete landing gear could be blown off in case of emergency landings. Especially on the Eastern Front many airstrips were in such a bad condition that nearly every day Stukas and other front-line aircraft were disabled as a result of broken undercarriages.

▲ 40

40. An aircraft of the 6th Staffel of Sturzkampfgeschwader 77 during the Luftschlacht um England, or Battle of Britain. The crew, an NCO and a Gefreiter, have just returned from a bloody mission over the British Isles and are telling other members of the squadron about the attacking Hurricanes. The aircraft is a Ju 87 B-2 which began its operational career during the summer of 1940. Early in 1941 the B-2 version made up half of all German Stuka Gruppen and soon overshadowed the B-1 in front-line service.

41. Ju 87D-1 Stukas of an unidentified Stukagruppe awaiting action with Heeresgruppe Mitte. The aircraft were equipped with four SC 50 bombs having a percussion detonator (Dinort-Spargel), additional Jericho-Trompeten and stabilizers fixed at the bomb's tail section. That kind of ordnance was often used against infantry units and Russian combined tank and infantry units, because the bombs exploded about two feet above the ground and had a great fragmentation effect.

42. An Italian truck (Autocarro leggiero SPA 38R) in front of one of the 155 Ju 87B-1, B-2, R-2 and other versions delivered to the Italian Air Force, early in the Second World War. Most of them were of the Ju 87B-2 and R-2 classes, the long-range Stuka, of which the Italian Air Force received 50 and 59 respectively during 1940. In 1943 they got an additional 46 Ju 87D-2 and D-3 which had the production numbers 7047 to 7098 and 8009 to 8058.

41 ▲ 42 ▼

▲ 43

43. Behind this SM.82 transport aircraft two Ju 82B-2s stand in front of wooden hangars at Lonante Pozzolo airfield. Nearly all the Italian Stukas were painted dark-green overall. These Stukas belonged to the 97th Gruppo Autonomo and

▼ 44

were engaged in several actions over the Mediterranean during November 1940 and the autumn of 1941. The Stuka became an essential part of the 'Addestramento Bombardamento' of the Italian Air Force.

44. Ju 87B-2s of the Italian Air Force in action over south-east Europe. The aircraft are carrying four GP bombs, and the structure behind the pilot's seat is fully armoured which gave the man at the controls additional security against

attacking fighters. The other crew man operated the single MG 15.

45. Italian Ju 87B-2 Stuka on parade in May 1941 when King Victor Emmanuel III was visiting his military units stationed in occupied Albania.

46. An aircraft of I./Stukageschwader 2 showing the Scotch Terrier on the front fuselage side, sported by all combat aircraft operated by the Stukagruppe. The terrier, named Molch, was the pet of the unit commander, Major Hitschold. The colour circles indicate the Staffel to which individual dive-bombers belonged. The aircraft of StG 2 had the code T6 and received the first of their brand-new Ju 87D-1s during January-February 1942.

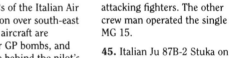

JUNKERS Ju 87 BASIC SPECIFICATION

Type	Ju 87A-1	Ju 87B-1	Ju 87C-1	Ju 87D-1	Ju 87D-8	Ju 87G-1
Wing Span	13.00m	13.20m	13.80m	13.80m	15.00m	13.80m
			5.00m folded			
Length	10.80m	11.00m	11.00m	11.00m	11.13m	11.00m
Height	3.90m	3.77m	3.77m	3.77m	3.84m	3.77m
Wing Area	30.00m^2	31.90m^2	31.90m^2	31.90m^2	32.60m^2	31.90m^2
Weight Empty	2273kg	2760kg	3655kg	2810kg	3800kg	3600kg
Loaded	3324kg	4400kg	5320kg	5720kg	6585kg	5100kg
Maximum Speed	320km/h	350km/h	344km/h	354km/h	400km/h	344km/h
Diving Speed	550km/h	600km/h	520km/h	600km/h	650km/h	–
Ceiling	9430m	8100m	9000m	9000m	7500m	7500m
Time of Climb	–	8.8min to 3000m	13.6min to 3000m	14.0min to 3000m	14.0min to 3000m	13.6min to 3000m
Range	995km	800km	1600km	1165km	1920km	1000km
Powerplant	Jumo 210D with 640hp/ 2700rpm	Jumo 211A with 1200hp/ 2300rpm	Jumo 211D with 1210hp/ 2300rpm	Jumo 211J with 1300hp/ 2600rpm	Jumo 211P with 1500hp 2600rpm	Jumo 211J with 1300hp/ 2600rpm
Bomb Load	max. 500 normal 250	1000kg	1000kg	1600kg	1800kg	no bomb load
Armament	1 fixed forward firing 7.9mm MG17 1 flexible 7.9mm MG15 rear	2 fixed forward firing 7.9mm MG17 1 flexible 7.9mm MG15 rear	2 fixed forward firing 7.9mm MG17 1 flexible 7.9mm MG15 rear	2 fixed forward firing 7.9mm MG17 1 flexible twin MG81Z rear	2 fixed forward firing 20mm MG151/20 1 flexible twin MG81Z rear	2 fixed forward firing 37mm Flak 18 1 flexible MG81Z rear

Ju 87A-1

Ju 87B-2

JUNKERS Ju 87 TYPES

Source: Flugzeugbaureihensblatt Ju 87; Chef TLR FL (E-2), 19 August 1944.

Type	Powerplant	Armament	Fuel (litres)	Radio	Remarks
Ju 87A-1	Jumo 210 D	1 MG 17 in wings; 1 flexible MG 15 rear; bomb load 500kg	480	FuG VII	Without armour.
Ju 87B-1	Jumo 211 A	2 MG 17 in wings; 1 flexible MG 15 rear; bomb load 1,000kg	480	FuG VIIa	Ski equipment, without armour.
Ju 87B-2	Jumo 211 D / Jumo 211 H	2 MG 17 in wings; 1 flexible MG 15 rear; bomb load 1,000kg	480	FuG VIIa	With armour, new undercarriage.
Ju 87C-1	Jumo 211 D	as Ju 87B-1	780 / 1,370	FuG 25 / Peil G6	Carrier dive-bomber with special equipment, underwing tank, five built.
Ju 87D-1	Jumo 211 J / Jumo 211 P	2 MG 17 in wings; 1 flexible twin MG81Z; bomb load 1,600kg	780 / 1,370	FuG 25 / Peil G6	Enlarged wings, ski equipment, glider-towing installation, new undercarriage and cooler.
Ju 87D-3	Jumo 211 J / Jumo 211 P	2 MG 17 in wings; 1 flexible twin MG81Z; bomb load 1,600kg	780 / 1,370	FuG 25 / Peil G6	Additional armour.
Ju 87D-4	Jumo 211 J	2 MG 151 in wings; 1 flexible twin MG81Z; 1 torpedo 750kg or 905kg	780 / 1,370	FuG 25 / Peil G6	Torpedo mount, modified Ju 87D-1 or D-3.
Ju 87D-5	Jumo 211 J / Jumo 211 P	2 MG 151 in wings; 1 flexible twin MG81Z; 1 torpedo 750kg or 905kg	780 / 1,370	FuG 25 / Peil G6	Enlarged wings.
Ju 87D-7	Jumo 211 J / Jumo 211 P	2 MG 151 in wings; 1 flexible twin MG81Z; bomb load 1,800kg	780 / 1,370	FuG 25 / Peil G6	As D-1, but wings of Ju 87D-5.
Ju 87D-8	Jumo 211 J / Jumo 211 P	2 MG 151 in wings; 1 flexible twin MG81Z; bomb load 1,800kg	780 / 1,370	FuG 25 / Peil G6	As D-3, but wings of Ju 87D-5 without Rüstsatzpanzerung.
Ju 87G-1	Jumo 211 J / Jumo 211 P	2 Flak 18 cannon; 1 flexible twin MG81Z; no bomb load	780	FuG 25 / Peil G6	Rebuilt D-3, without dive-brakes, only tank-busting role.
Ju 87G-2	Jumo 211 J / Jumo 211 P	2 Flak 18 cannon; 1 flexible twin MG81Z; no bomb load	780	FuG 25 / Peil G6	Rebuilt D-5, without dive-brakes, only tank-busting role.
Ju 87H-1	Jumo 211 J / Jumo 211 P	no weapons			Rebuilt D-1, trainer, dual controls and seating.
Ju 87H-3	Jumo 211 J / Jumo 211 P	no weapons			Rebuilt D-3, trainer, dual controls and seating.
Ju 87H-5	Jumo 211 J / Jumo 211 P	no weapons			Rebuilt D-5, trainer, dual controls and seating.
Ju 87H-7	Jumo 211 J / Jumo 211 P	no weapons			Rebuilt D-7, trainer, dual controls and seating.
Ju 87H-8	Jumo 211 J / Jumo 211 P	no weapons			Rebuilt D-8, trainer, dual controls and seating.
Ju 87K-1	Jumo 210 D	as Ju 87A-1			As A-1, for export to Japan.
Ju 87K-2	Jumo 211 D	as Ju 87B-1			As B-1, for export to Hungary.
Ju 87K-4	Jumo 210 D	as Ju 87A-1			As A-1, for export to Hungary.
Ju 87R-1	Jumo 211 A	as Ju 87B-1	780 / 1,370	FuG 25 / Peil G6	Underwing tanks on outer wing bomb-rack, extended range as B-1.
Ju 87R-2	Jumo 211 D / Jumo 211 H	as Ju 87B-2	780 / 1,370	FuG 25 / Peil G6	Underwing drop tanks on outer wing bomb-racks, extended range.
Ju 87R-4	Jumo 211 D / Jumo 211 H	as Ju 87B-2	780 / 1,370	FuG 25 / Peil G6	Special weapons packs (SG – Behälter).

Ju 87D-3

Ju 87G-2

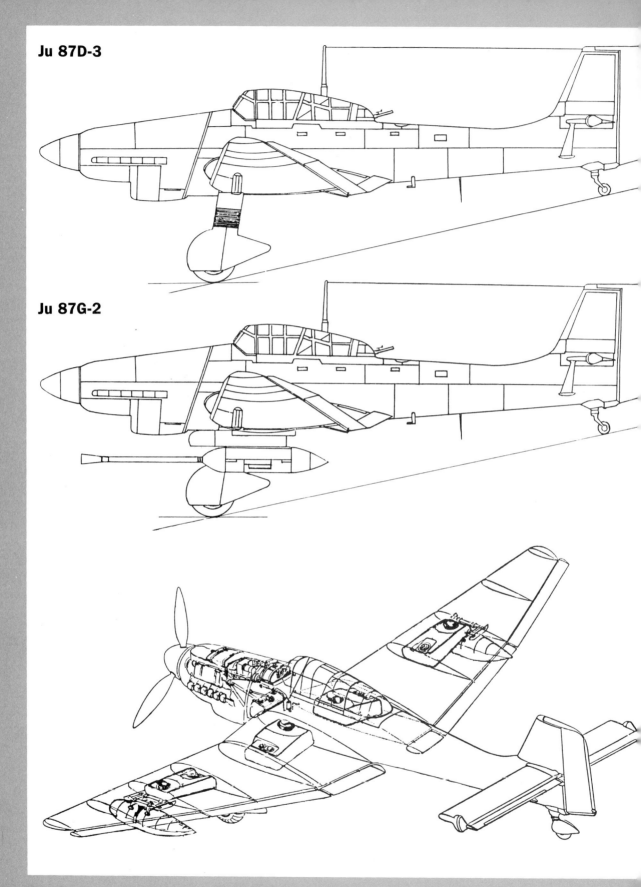

STUKA UNITS AND DEPLOYMENT

Source: Ing. Preusdiken.

Unit	Establishment	Operational Theatre			Remarks
StG 162	1 October 1935				Establishment: Schwerin. Became StG 2 in April 1939.
StG 165	1 March 1936				Establishment: Schweinfurt. Became III./StG 51 in 1939. Parts became I. and II./StG 77.
StG 1	1 October 1939	September	1939	Poland	Became SG 1 in October 1943.
		April	1940	Norway	Equipped with Fw 190.
		February	1941	Mediterranean	
		January	1943	Northern Russia	
StG 2	1 May 1939	September	1939	Poland	Became SG 2 in October 1943.
		June	1940	France	Equipped with Fw 190.
		January	1941	Greece	
		June	1941	South Russia	
StG 3	Autumn 1940	August	1940	Battle of Britain	Became SG 3 in October 1943.
		January	1941	Greece	Equipped with Fw 190.
		January	1942	Mediterranean	
StG 5	Summer 1942	July	1942	Finland	Became SG 5 in October 1943.
		November	1943	Northern Russia	Equipped with Fw 190 in June 1944.
		December	1943	Southern Russia	
		January	1944	Northern Russia	
		April	1944	Finland	
StG 51	Summer 1939	September	1939	Poland	I. + II./StG 51 became II./StG 77 in 1939, III./StG 51 became II./StG 1 in Autumn 1940.
		End of 1939		Western Europe (Only III./StG 51)	
StG 76	Summer 1939	September	1939	Poland	Only one Gruppe established; became I./StG 3 in Autumn 1940.
		End of	1939	Western Europe	
		May	1940	France	
StG 77	Summer 1939	September	1939	Poland	II./StG 77 became I./SG 10 in October 1943, I. + III./StG 77. Re-equipped with Fw 190.
		May	1940	France	
		August	1940	Battle of Britain	
		June	1941	Russia	
StG 101	Summer 1943	—			Became SG 103 in October 1943 (Training Unit only).
StG 102	Summer 1943	—			Became SG 102 in October 1943 (Training Unit only).
StG 103	October 1943	—			Personnel became part of the SS Brigade Westphalia.
StG 151	Summer 1943	Croatia			
Trägergrp. 186	1 October 1938	—			Became III./StG 1 in 1940.

▲ 47

47. By the spring of 1942 Sturzkampfgeschwader StG 3 had absorbed I. Gruppe of StG 1 as its second Gruppe, and II./StG 2 as its third Gruppe. Perhaps this aircraft, displaying a giraffe and standing in front of a wall of cactus, belonged to one of these units; the large radiator of the Ju 87B-2 bears instructions for the mixture required to protect against frost.

48. The rare Ju 87B-2/U4 conversion package offered a logical solution to operations from snowbound airfields in Russia. Because the dive-bomber's speed suffered, its usage did not become widespread in the Luftwaffe. Nevertheless the ski equipment remained an option on subsequent Ju 87 variants. Together with the He 111 and the Junkers Ju 88 bomber, this arrangement was evaluated by the E-Stelle Rechlin.

49. To improve the poor range of the Ju 87B-1/B-2, the Ju 87R-1/R-2 featured an additional fuel transfer system and the ability to carry two standard 300-litre drop tanks in place of the outer bomb racks under the wings. The designation 'R' stood for Reichweite (range). When drop tanks were not required for long-range missions the Ju 87R could be rigged to carry the normal load under the outer wings without major modifications.

50. Late production, or rebuilt, Stukas used the standard Ju 87B-2 airframe. All external details between B-2 and R-2 were identical, but the maximum weight could be raised to more than 3,550kg. The maximum range of the heavier Ju 87R-2 was rated below that of the R-1, having a range of only 780 miles. This fact did not inhibit the Ju 87R-2's operational career after its début over the Mediterranean early in 1941.

51. A Ju 87R-1 just before handing over to the Italian Air Force. On the antenna can be seen the instruction 'Nicht anfassen!' (Don't touch!).

▲ 48　▼ 49

 ▲ 52 ▼ 53

54 ▲   55 ▼

52. It was suggested that Junkers Ju 87 dive-bombers be carried aboard the sole German aircraft carrier *Graf Zeppelin*, and later on aboard other carriers which were planned by Naval HQ. In December 1938 the newly activated dive-bomber carrier Gruppe was equipped with some Ju 87s, but only for training purposes. With the introduction of the improved Ju 87B-1/B-2, a special naval version, Ju 87C, was constructed.

53. The wings of the sea Stuka could be folded back manually for shipboard storage. Some additional modifications were necessary, e.g., a catapult gear, an arresting hook under the rear fuselage and air bags in case of ditching. The wing span was shortened also.

54, 55. Two close-ups of the simple tail-box attachment point which was common to all Ju 87 glider-tugs. The external tubular mounting frame was fastened at the after fuselage bulkheads and could be installed by all Luftwaffe Feldwerften without great effort. Normally the Ju 87B/R was used for towing the DFS 230 glider, and smaller aircraft were towed during pilots' initial training.

56. During March and April 1939 the first two Ju 87s were ready for converting to Ju 87C prototypes. During the following summer the Berlin Tempelhof production line handed over a pre-series of ten Ju 87C-O to the Luftwaffe. The navalized dive-bombers were flown to 4./Trägergruppe 186 for service evaluation and crew training. After the carrier *Graf Zeppelin*, however, for various reasons production of aircraft for the carrier remained at a standstill until the end of the war.

57. Only a few Ju 87 C-1 were rebuilt using standard Ju 87B-2 airframes. Despite the cancellation of the Ju 87C programme, many evaluation trials were carried out by Luftwaffe E-Stellen on the orders of Supreme Command which stated that the large carrier would see active service in 1942. After the failure to finish the carrier, the fourth Trägerstaffel 186 was brought to active strength as Stukagruppe, (StGr) 186. In July 1940 that unit became part of III./StG 1. The crews retained their anchor and helmet unit symbol on their Ju 87 aircraft.

58. After the end of the Polish campaign, the weak defensive armament of the Ju 87B-1/B-2 was criticized. The next large series was the Ju 87D of which the first prototype was the Ju 87V21. Due to problems with the Jumo 211 F piston engine, more months of evaluation were needed. The main changes focused on the nose, the two-seat canopy and an improved undercarriage which could be jettisoned in an emergency.

59. This Ju 87D-1 has its entire cooling system and engine cover removed for maintenance. The front of the fuselage was aero-dynamically reconfigured and seemed a little longer. The necessary oil cooler had to have a shallow bath on the cowling's underside. This aircraft was one of Sturzkampfgeschwader 2.

▲ 56 ▼ 57

▲ 60

▲ 61 ▼ 62

60. Four Ju 87D-3 of Stukageschwader 2, with the unit's code T6, seen over the wide Russian landscape in 1943. The 'Dora 3' took part at the fateful battle of Kursk, destroying many Russian tanks with small bombs in co-operation with the tank-hunters. The Ju 87D-2 and D-3 were increasingly used for low-level ground attacks and were given more and more internal and external armour protection.

61. Both new coolant radiators under the main wing section indicates that this Stuka would belong either to D-1, D-2 or D-3 version. In comparison with the Ju 87B the centreline ETC was modified too. The rack was streamline-covered, and all Ju 87Ds were equipped with two pairs of racks under the wings. There were ordnance options of carrying Abwurfbehälter AB 250 or AB 500 (wooden dispenser), the mentioned WB 81 with six MG 81 guns, different all-purpose containers or flares and smoke-discharger tubes.

62. The Ju 87V22 is thought to have been the second prototype of the D-1 series built by Junkers. The undercarriage was strengthened to accommodate increased maximum weight. The early and late JU 87D-1s differed from each other by having a siren mount fitted. In their role as low-attack aircraft the sirens were later removed by the Luftwaffe.

63. On 6 February 1944 Sonderführer Zwirner, serving with a PK company on the North-eastern Front, photographed this Ju 87D5 which has a glider towing installation and two heavy 20mm MG 151/20 in the wings. The aircraft was probably used for towing the DFS 230 loaded with essential equipment in the event of a sudden transfer to another airfield.

64. Only a few of these warming and repair tents were delivered to Luftwaffe units in Russia, despite a great lack of hangars for repairing aircraft.

63 ▲ 64 ▼

▲ 65   ▼ 66

65. At the Graf Zeppelin research institute at Stuttgart-Ruit, overwing pod trials were conducted using a Klemm 35 and a Ju 87D-3. Two of these detachable pods, each seating two men, were fixed between the outer bomb racks and the wing armament. The idea was a bid to solve the problem of shortage of transport aircraft, if an airfield had to be vacated in a hurry.

66. One of the Ju 87D-3s during the Battle of Kursk. The advance, Operation 'Zitadelle', was supported by strong elements of VIII Fliegerkorps (with parts of Luftflotte 4) and I Fliegerkorps (with Luftflotte 1). Together, the two units totalled 1,830 aircraft, including all three Gruppen of Sturtzkampfgeschwader 1.

67. A Ju 87D-1 seen while loading a huge SC 1000 GP bomb on the Eastern Front. The block-and-tackle and its ropes are lying in front of the dive-bomber. Bombs like this were used by the combined forces of VIII Fliegerkorps for demolishing enemy strong points such as warships in the Black Sea, and the large fortifications at Sevastapol.

68. The Ju 87D-1, coded BK+EF, later became a prototype for the D-4 development, a torpedo-carrying Ju 87 bomber, with a rack-mounted 1,687lb LT F5b torpedo under the fuselage. After trials were made with He 111, Do 217 and Ju 88 torpedo-bombers there was no chance to realize a Ju 87 LT version, because the endurance and performance of the aircraft were inadequate.

67 ▲   68 ▼

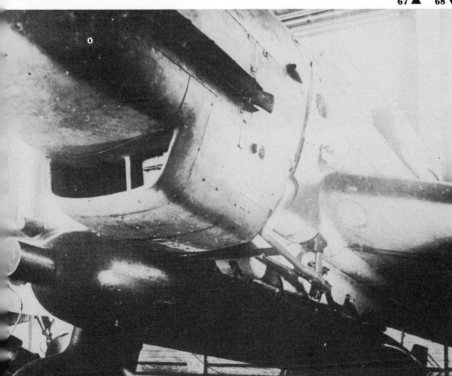

▲ 69 ▼ 70

69. To improve the range of the LT bombers two 300litre drop tanks were fixed under the wings of the Ju 87D-4. Most of the necessary trials were carried out at Grosseto in Italy, one of the Axis centres for torpedo development and evaluation. Other tests were carried out at Gotenhafen on the Baltic.

70. Another view of the BK+EF at Grosseto, with one Ubungstorpedo (exercise torpedo) under the fuselage.

71. It was proposed to produce a first batch of 115 Ju 87E-1 torpedo-bombers as the aircraft complement for the carrier *Graf Zeppelin* and the merchant ships which were supposed to become a Hilfsflugzeugträger. After the Ju 87D-4, the derivative Ju 87E-1 was to get the special seaborne equipment needed for operations from ships such as the arrester hook.

72, 73. As well as the experimental versions with personnel pods, flame-throwers and weapons under the wings, some Ju 87B and D were used for evaluation trials with new cooling and dust filter systems fitted by Junkers and Daimler-Benz. This aircraft, seen at Nabern near Kirchheim/Teck in southern Germany, may have been one of the experimental testbeds flown by Daimler-Benz at the nearby Stuttgart–Echterdingen airfield.

71 ▲

72 ▲ 73 ▼

▲ 74   ▼ 75

74. In a last effort at refining the Ju 87 Stuka and improving its ground-attack capabilities, the Junkers Ju 87D-5 was designed and introduced into production early in 1943. The fuselage was nearly identical with its predecessors, but the wingspan was lengthened. The wing machine-guns (MG 17) of the Ju 87D-5 were replaced by the more powerful 20mm MG 151/20. The siren's mounting was deleted, there being no further need of them.

75. A Ju 87D-5 ground-attack aircraft on the Eastern front in November 1944. At this time only a few Staffeln flew the Stuka, for example elements of StG 1, StG 2, StG 77 and Schlachtgeschwader 9. Most of the early Stuka Staffeln had been equipped with the faster Fw 190 F and G ground-attack aircraft.

76, 77. Two views taken during the Tragschlepp (towing) development of the Deutsche Forschungsanstalt für Segelflug at Neuburg in Bavaria. One Ju 87B-2 was towed beneath a Heinkel He 111H-6 (code SG+ KA) belonging to the DFS in Ainring near Salzburg in Austria. The Junkers had the civil code number D-ABUT until the end of the war. Later, adequate trials were flown with a Bachem BP 20 Natter to evaluate the gliding behaviour of that small rocket-propelled interceptor aircraft.

▲ 78

▲ 79 ▼ 80

78. Colonel Ernst Kupfer, the famous commander of Sturzkampfgeschwader 2, standing on the wing of a Ju 87D-1 with additional armour on both sides of the cockpit.

79. This ground crew member has just checked the interior weapons compartment of a Ju 87D-5 belonging to an unidentified unit on the Eastern Front. The Ju 87D-5 was in widespread use with Sturzkampfgeschwader and Schlachtgeschwader SG 1, 2, 3, 5 and 77 until most of the Ju 87s were replaced by the Focke-Wulf Fw 190 F.

80. A close-up of the rear defence position with its MG 81Z and the Peil GIV (Peilgerät direction-finding radar) just behind the cockpit.

81. Harmonizing the big 3.7cm anti-tank guns on a range in Germany. The Ju 87G-1 and G-2 were both armed with two of . these Flak 18 which had been developed up to 1935 by Rheinmetal-Borsig as a light anti-tank gun. Later it was widely installed in the Ju 88P, Bf 110 and the Hs 129. In addition to its role as a heavy aircraft destroyer, the gun saw widespread action against Russian tank armies.

82. One of the early Ju 87G-1 just before handing over to Panzerjagdkommando Weiss on the Eastern Front. There were two major versions of the Ju 87G, recognizable by the short wing span (G-1) and the long span (G-2). Both tank-busters, also called Kanonenvogel or Panzerknacker, were armed with the same two guns, each having six-round clips of armour-penetrating tungsten-core shells.

81 ▲   82 ▼

▲ 83 ▼ 84 ▼ 85

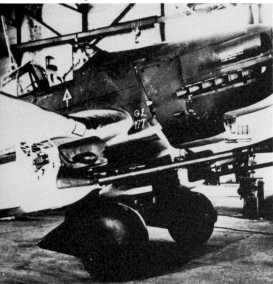

83. An aircraft of Panzerjagdkommando Weiss having its Jumo 211 engine started by two men of the ground crew in February 1943 when the success enjoyed by such small units began. Most of the pilots were selected veteran Stuka fliers and had large experience of, and great skill with, that type of aircraft. After its evaluation, most of the Ju 87G-1 were issued to Sturzkampfgeschwader 1 and 2 and, late in 1943, to Schlachtgeschwader 3 and 77.

84. A Ju 87G-2, a modification of the standard Ju 87D-5. Of the final production order for 208 modified tank-busters, about 180 were produced at Bremen–Lemwerden before all Ju 87 manufacturing ceased in October 1944. This Ju 87G-2 had the production number '177' painted near the wing roots, together with the designation of the new conversion.

86 ▲

85. One of the rare tank-busters equipped with flame dampers, after its capture by American ground forces early in May 1945. Due to the interest of the 'new management' some of the coverings of the anachronistic Stuka have been opened. Normally only the Ju 87D-7 and D-8, both rebuilt Ju 87D-3 and D-5, of the Störkampfstaffeln had the large flame damper.

86, 87. Two views of a captured Ju 87G-2 which is being examined by Allied specialists after the crew had surrendered the tank-buster on an American-occupied airfield in western Germany at the end of April 1945.

87 ▲   **88** ▼

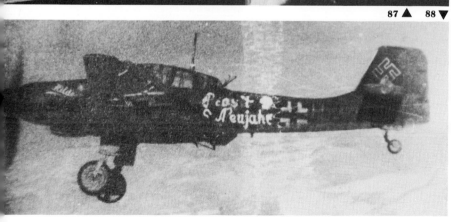

88. Despite its poor quality, this is an interesting photograph of a Ju 87D-1 without undercarriage spats. Flying over a snowy landscape, the ground crew wish friend and foe a happy New Year. There is no indication of when the picture was taken, but it was possibly during the winter of 1943–4.

▲ 89

▲ 90 ▼ 91

89. Allied troops examine this Ju 87D-5 of an unidentified Stuka unit, bearing the production number 8502. In the background is one of many captured Ju 88G-1 night-fighters abandoned on airfields by the end of the war.

90. This Ju 87D-8 was equipped with a large 600litre drop tank. Possibly the empty canister was used for transportation of important tools and spare parts.

91. A Stuka night-fighter with large transportation canister beneath the centreline rack, seen at a Western air base towards the end of the war.

92. After the unconditional surrender of Germany on 8 May 1945, many serviceable and partly destroyed Luftwaffe aircraft were scattered all over Germany. This Ju 87D-8 was one of the modified D-5 aircraft with flame dampers and a late version of the D/F loop near the antenna. In the background is a Ju 88G-6 heavy night-fighter with SN 2 radar.

93. On 8 May 1945 this Stuka crew surrendered with their Ju 87G-2 which had brought them from their Luftflotte 6 operational area to one of the Western Allies' forward airstrips. All important parts of the defensive armament and the main parts of both Flak 18 had been removed before the Ju 87's last flight.

94. After landing near Magdeburg the crews destroyed these Ju 87D-8s with hand-grenades to deny them to Allied forces. In the foregound is a wrecked Ju 88G with the production number 6233?? which identifies the night-fighter as a late G-6 version with SN 2 anti-aircraft radar equipment.

92 ▲

93 ▲   94 ▼

The *Fotofax* series

A new range of pictorial studies of military subjects for the modeller, historian and enthusiast. Each title features a carefully-selected set of photographs plus a data section of facts and figures on the topic covered. With line drawings and detailed captioning, every volume represents a succinct and valuable study of the subject. New and forthcoming titles:

Warbirds
F-111 Aardvark
P-47 Thunderbolt
B-52 Stratofortress
Stuka!
Jaguar
US Strategic Air Power:
  Europe 1942–1945
Dornier Bombers
RAF in Germany

Vintage Aircraft
German Naval Air Service
Sopwith Camel
Fleet Air Arm, 1920–1939
German Bombers of WWI

Soldiers
World War One: 1914
World War One: 1915
World War One: 1916
Union Forces of the American
  Civil War
Confederate Forces of the
  American Civil War
Luftwaffe Uniforms
British Battledress 1945–1967
  (2 vols)

Warships
Japanese Battleships, 1897–
  1945
Escort Carriers of World War
  Two
German Battleships, 1897–
  1945
Soviet Navy at War, 1941–1945
US Navy in World War Two,
  1943–1944
US Navy, 1946–1980 (2 vols)
British Submarines of World
  War One

Military Vehicles
The Chieftain Tank
Soviet Mechanized Firepower
  Today
British Armoured Cars since
  1945
NATO Armoured Fighting
  Vehicles
The Road to Berlin
NATO Support Vehicles

The *Illustrated* series

The internationally successful range of photo albums devoted to current, recent and historic topics, compiled by leading authors and representing the best means of obtaining your own photo archive.

Warbirds
US Spyplanes
USAF Today
Strategic Bombers, 1945–1985
Air War over Germany
Mirage
US Naval and Marine Aircraft
  Today
USAAF in World War Two
B-17 Flying Fortress
Tornado
Junkers Bombers of World War
  Two
Argentine Air Forces in the
  Falklands Conflict
F-4 Phantom Vol II
Army Gunships in Vietnam
Soviet Air Power Today
F-105 Thunderchief
Fifty Classic Warbirds
Canberra and B-57
German Jets of World War Two

Vintage Warbirds
The Royal Flying Corps in
  World War One
German Army Air Service in
  World War One
RAF between the Wars
The Bristol Fighter
Fokker Fighters of World War
  One
Air War over Britain, 1914–
  1918
Nieuport Aircraft of World War
  One

Tanks
Israeli Tanks and Combat
  Vehicles
Operation Barbarossa
Afrika Korps
Self-Propelled Howitzers
British Army Combat Vehicles
  1945 to the Present
The Churchill Tank
US Mechanized Firepower
  Today
Hitler's Panzers
Panzer Armee Afrika
US Marine Tanks in World War
  Two

Warships
The Royal Navy in 1980s
The US Navy Today
NATO Navies of the 1980s
British Destroyers in World
  War Two
Nuclear Powered Submarines
Soviet Navy Today
British Destroyers in World
  War One
The World's Aircraft Carriers,
  1914–1945
The Russian Convoys, 1941–
  1945
The US Navy in World War
  Two
British Submarines in World
  War Two
British Cruisers in World War
  One
U-Boats of World War Two
Malta Convoys, 1940–1943

Uniforms
US Special Forces of World
  War Two
US Special Forces 1945 to the
  Present
The British Army in Northern
  Ireland
Israeli Defence Forces, 1948 to
  the Present
British Special Forces, 1945 to
  Present
US Army Uniforms Europe,
  1944–1945
The French Foreign Legion
Modern American Soldier
Israeli Elite Units
US Airborne Forces of World
  War Two
The Boer War
The Commandos World War
  Two to the Present
Victorian Colonial Wars

A catalogue listing these series and other Arms & Armour Press titles is available on request from: Sales Department, Arms & Armour Press, Artillery House, Artillery Row, London SW1P 1RT.